TABLE OF CONTENTS

GIRLS WANTS TO BE SMART

Does every teenage girl desire to be intelligent? Yes, but being a smart teen goes beyond wise decisions both in day-to-day living and while establishing future plans. Let's go somewhere; as a teenage girl, you should be aware of this
The first thing to do is set aside time for studying. Seeking balance is good since most people may feel fulfilled when their lives are balanced. Although it can be challenging, balancing your time is possible. Investigate your passions, interests, and relationships, but watch out that they don't

interfere with your academic work.

In order to keep track of everything, create a homework schedule.

Participate in class, second. While it may not always be easy to speak up in class, doing so can help you engage with the subject matter and gain knowledge from your lecturers and peers.

You will feel more engaged, self-assured, and capable if you raise your hand.

Sometimes getting incorrect answers is acceptable. All intelligent students do it; it's an essential part of studying, and your classmates won't really notice.

Thirdly, seek assistance when required. The most diligent pupils perform the best, therefore developing a strong work ethic. Find a helper if you are unable to solve a problem on your own.

To ask a question in class, raise your hand.

Outside of class, speak with your tutor or teacher.

Ask a parent, friend, or sibling who is older to explain an idea to you.

You need to get enough sleep. Nobody who is exhausted and burned out can perform at their best. Take breaks from studying and schoolwork to get some rest, and schedule study sessions in between extended periods of concentration.

Keep your stress in check, girl. Everyone requires a break from work or education. Make time for your favorite healthy "de-stressors," whatever they may be. Make time for whatever you

I need to help you deal with stress, whether it's joining a sports team, practicing yoga, going hiking, reading, creating art, or watching a good movie.

You should establish wholesome behaviors. It's simple to put your health and hygiene aside, but making healthy habits a priority now will set you up for a healthy future and is generally a wise decision. Exercise frequently, eat healthily, and practice good cleanliness.

Ask for opinions on your most important decisions. Nobody has all the answers, but getting advice from your parents and role models can go a long way toward helping teens make wise decisions. They will always be aware of what to do. No. However, they might be able to offer you advice as you grapple with tough choices, especially if they've been in your shoes before. Be receptive to suggestions from others to guide you in making wise decisions in both your daily life and future planning.

Recognize that making mistakes is a necessary part of learning. All intelligent people err. They are still intelligent despite this. Working hard is what matters in the long run, and getting back up after a setback will be beneficial for you.

Just hold off picking up for the wise you.

MY WORKOUT ROUTINE

Many young girls turn their backs on sports and fitness

when it comes to teenage girls and exercise.

exercising every day for an hour

Only 10% of girls between the ages of 14 and 16 engage in the recommended level of physical activity due to pressures from exams, social life, hormones, body consciousness, and a host of other conflicting factors. This amounts to one hour of exercise per day, per the NHS. Even though this may seem like a lot, it could also include short bouts of exercise spread throughout the day, like walking or cycling to school. For instance, a morning 15-minute walk or run, a 30-minute PE lesson at school, and an evening 15-minute yoga session.

According to research by the Women's Sport and Fitness Foundation, 51% of secondary school-aged girls say their experiences in physical education and school sports have discouraged them from participating in sports.

Any number of diverse factors may be to blame for this.

Teenage girls want to try sports other than the traditional ones taught in schools, while some complain that the competition in the activities is too intense. Others, meanwhile, are very self-conscious about their required PE gear.

badminton courts in a sports facility

Girls can select their athletic attire for the gym setting. When elite-level girls and women were informed that they could not compete in international basketball competitions while wearing the hijab, one prominent basketball player and spoken word artist, Asma Elbadawi, took to the airwaves with a poem highlighting the issue of sports equipment. She argued that this was discriminatory toward a specific group of people, but her larger point was that wearing skimpy PE attire could make people feel extremely uneasy. Many teenagers struggle with body image at this age, so who wants to wear such clothing?

In the gym, there is something for everyone.

We provide a wide variety of classes and activities, which is important. Many girls just want to maintain their fitness levels as teenagers. The best exercise for this would be a typical gym workout that focused on cardiovascular activity while using some light weights. However, it is also beneficial for teenagers to enroll in classes like spin, boxercise, yoga, or circuits to add variety and broaden their knowledge. Teenagers looking for a different challenge are often very interested in activities like climbing.

Teens who are competitive can work as hard as they want in the gym, of course. The best advice on how to prepare for a sport is always available from personal trainers and gym instructors to aspiring athletes and team members.

avoiding the discomforts of adolescence

It's important to note that many young girls will experience drops in energy levels as a result of raging hormones. Osgood-Schlatter disease is a possibility to develop. When the joints and muscles in the legs are overworked, this happens. In order to prevent teenagers from going overboard, parents and caregivers should work with them.

Teenage girls' extracurriculars ought to consist of:

Strength training with your own body weight can help you develop strong bones, ligaments, and tendons.

Increase your stamina and metabolism with endurance sports like running, cycling, and swimming.

Yoga, dance, and gymnastics can help you stay flexible during the body's period of rapid growth.

coordinating motions in jumps, catches, and throws.

Positive feedback from peers, family, and friends is crucial because girls are likely to feel extremely self-conscious during this time. A positive body image must be formed during the teenage years. The development of strong bones is also crucial during this period of life. The teenage years are when a woman's peak bone mass is deposited, at 90%. Therefore, physical activity is essential at this age to ensure strong, healthy bones in the future.

a means of reducing tension in adolescents

At this point, teenagers are under a lot of pressure. Stress can be reduced by exercising. It causes endorphin release and increases confidence. It works well to combat the issues brought on by puberty, such as erratic moods, a lack of motivation, and depleted energy.

A visit to the gym might be the unanticipated solution if you are a teen who is having life problems.

HOW MUCH DO I NEED SLEEP?

Most teenagers require between 8 and 10 hours in sports to get the recommended amount of sleep every night. Unfortunately, a lot of teenagers lack adequate sleep.

Why Do Teens Sleep So Little?

Teenagers frequently received a bad rap for sleeping in class, staying up late, and oversleeping for assignments. However, teen sleep habits differ from those of adults or younger children.

The circadian rhythm, or internal biological clock, in a person's body, is reset during the teen years, causing them to sleep and wake up later. Melatonin, a brain hormone, is released later in the night in teens than in children and adults, which may be the cause of this change. Teenagers may find it more challenging to get to sleep early as a result.

Changes in the circadian rhythm of the body occur during a busy period of life. For the majority of teenagers, the pressure to perform well in school is greater, and it is more difficult to get by without working hard to study. Teenagers also have other time commitments, such as participating in extracurricular activities, working a part-time job, and participating in sports. It is also challenging to get to sleep when using electronics, such as computers, tablets, and phones. Teenagers frequently stay up late sending texts, playing games, and watching videos.

Early school start times also contribute to a lack of sleep. Teenagers who stay up late still need to wake up early for school, so they might only get 6 or 7 hours of sleep per night, at most. Even though it might not seem like much, a few hours less sleep each night adds up to a definite sleep deficit over time.

Why Is Sleep Vital?

For you to function at your best, sleep is essential. Teens must sleep to:

learn in class by paying attention.

better one's athletic performance

develop normally, be healthy, and grow

Poor grades, relationship issues, and drowsy driving can

result from lack of sleep. Serious car accidents can result from falling asleep at the wheel.

People with persistent sleep issues may have:

Obesity and heart disease are examples of health issues.

infection resistance issues

with emotion, such as depression

How Much Sleep Am I Getting?

Even if you believe you are getting enough sleep, this may not be the case. You might require more rest if you:

have a difficult time getting out of bed have trouble focusing are nodding off in class feel agitated, moody, depressed, or sad

How can I sleep more soundly?

Here are some suggestions for improving your sleep:

Establish regular bedtimes and wake-up times. Even on weekends, try to adhere to your sleep routine to the nearest hour or two.

Regularly moving around. Sleeping better can be aided by regular exercise. However, avoid working out immediately before bed. It may be difficult to fall asleep after an intense workout.

Beware of caffeine. After dinner, stay away from caffeinated drinks like soda, tea, and coffee. In the evening, alcohol and nicotine (from smoking or vaping) might awaken a person and prevent them from falling asleep.

Dim the lights to help you relax. The brain receives a wake-up signal from light. Your body can unwind by avoiding bright lights, including those from electronic devices, listening to calming music, or practicing meditation before bed.

electronic devices off. One hour or more before bedtime, avoid using your phone (including texting), tablet, computer, or TV.

Limit your napping. Longer daytime naps and naps taken too close to bedtime may prevent you from falling asleep later.

Make your bedroom a comfortable place to sleep.

Dark, slightly chilly surroundings are ideal for sleeping. If you need to block out a noisy environment, use a white noise or nature sounds machine or app.

BUILDING A HYGIENE ROUTINE

Every teenage girl wants to be hygienic, but some girls don't know where to start.

Shower, wash or bathe every day. Showering, washing, or bathing keeps you clean and fresh smelling, so even if you don't feel like it, remember to clean your whole body every day. Make sure to wash your feet well and your armpits.

Consider removing hair from your legs, face, armpits, or any other part of your body you think needs to be hairless to be hygienic. Body hair is not unhygienic, men have it, and a lot of them are hygienic! You don't have to shave to be hygienic. It is a very personal thing, you should shave whenever you think it's time to

and, whatever you think you should shave,. Use
shaving cream or soap - never try to shave without shaving cream or soap, as it can lead to irritation, nicks, and little red bumps, which you don't want.
If you want any part of your body to be hairless, you can wax, thread, epilate, pluck or use hair removal creams
You can apply oil to remove wax from the skin.
It helps to reduce the stickiness of wax.
Have good oral hygiene. Clean your teeth, and use floss. Use mouthwash, and see a dentist regularly. Keep your breath fresh.
Consider wearing deodorant or antiperspirant every day. Smelling good does not make you hygienic, but, if you smell bad, you may have a hygiene issue. If you wash the sweat from your body before it becomes stale and stinky, you can consider yourself hygienic. This is very practical though, using antiperspirant so you don't sweat. You can also wear perfume, eau de cologne, eau

de toilette, scented moisturizer, or body spray to smell fragrant - this is optional.

Wear clean clothes. There is no point in having a hygienic body if you dress in dirty clothes - it'll just make you stink and look unkempt.

Wash your hair whenever you feel that it's necessary. Washing your hair every day will strip your hair and scalp of the natural oils it needs to stay hydrated. Use shampoo made especially for your hair type, and never skip conditioner. You can also straighten or curl if you want but the look of your hair has absolutely nothing to do with how clean you are.

Trim your nails so that dirt does not build up under them. Do not bite, lick or pick at your nails. Nail polish is optional, but try not to paint your nails more than twice a month, as this can lead to the yellowing and weakening of your nails which whilst not unhygienic is unsightly.

Keep your face hygienic. Gentle soap and water and never going to bed with makeup on are enough to have a hygienic face. If you're interested in looking after the appearance of the skin on your face beyond hygiene you can

Use a cleanser recommended for your skin type. Put a small amount of face cleanser on your hands, about the size of a nickel, and rub some on your wet hands. Use a product that is gentle enough for your skin, because something too strong will just dry the skin out and stimulate the oil glands to produce more oil - you're trying to remove oil and retain moisture at the same time. Do not use soap - it's too strong, and can't be rinsed easily.

Using your fingertips, massage the cleanser all over your face, removing any dirt and oil. Take thirty seconds or so, concentrating on first the hairline, then paying special attention to the "T-zone" (forehead, nose, and nostril area), then around the mouth and chin, then cheeks. Cleanse the neck using upward strokes. You have oil glands behind your ears, so don't neglect that area. It's messy but do it anyway. When you're fifty, you will be glad you went to the trouble to help your mature skin look its best. Rinse your face with warm water and pat it dry with a soft towel.

Moisturizer is a very good thing. You have just washed off dirt and oil, and a moisturizer will help keep the moisture in the surface cells, which promotes a more youthful-looking complexion - plus it feels great.

Adopt healthy habits. Wash your hands before eating. Don't pick your nose. Keep piercings clean. Don't pick scabs. Wash your hands after going to the toilet, every single time. Always use cover your mouth when you cover and always sneeze into a tissue or handkerchief. Never spit. Keep your body free of unhygienic substances. Change your clothes whenever they become soiled.

Teenagers
As you get older, you have more freedom to decide for yourself about many of the issues that are most important to you. You can pick your own pals, music, and attire. You might also be prepared to make choices regarding your physical well-being.
Making wise choices about your diet and drinking habits, level of activity, and amount of sleep is a fantastic place to start. You can discover more here.
how your body functions
how your body utilizes the food and beverages you ingest, as well as how exercise may aid in calorie "burning"
how to pick wholesome foods and beverages
How to Get Moving and Stay Active How to Plan Healthy Meals and Physical Activities That Fit Your Lifestyle How to Establish and Maintain Healthy Habits How to Get

Enough Sleep How to Establish and Maintain Healthy Habits
For even more practical advice and suggestions, don't forget to look at the "Did you know?" boxes.

Did you realize?
In children between the ages of 12 and 19, obesity affects about 20% of them. However, making minor adjustments to your food and exercise routines may help you achieve and maintain a healthy weight.

The body uses energy in what ways?
Your body requires energy to grow and function. You get that energy from the calories in meals and beverages. Consider food as the energy you need to get through the day. You need to eat and drink to be fueled throughout the day since you need the battery's energy to think and move. "Energy balance" refers to the harmony between the energy you obtain from food and drink and the energy you expend for development, activity, and daily living. Maintaining a

healthy weight may be made easier by energy balance.

For your body to work, you need energy. You get that energy from the calories in meals and beverages.

What calorie requirements does your body have?

Calories required to maintain a healthy weight or to be active vary depending on the individual. The number of calories you require is influenced by your gender, genetics, age, height, weight, if you are still growing, and level of activity, which may vary from day to day.

How should your weight be controlled or managed?

Some teenagers attempt weight loss by eating very little, eliminating entire food groups—such as those high in carbohydrates—skipping meals, or even fasting. These methods of weight loss may be dangerous because they could exclude vital nutrients that your body requires. In reality, poor dieting may hinder attempts to control weight since it can result in a vicious cycle of under-eating followed by overeating as a result of hunger. Unhealthy dieting may also have an impact on how you feel and develop.

Using laxatives or diet medications to lose weight, smoking, or forcing yourself to vomit can all have negative health effects. If you force yourself to vomit, take laxatives or diet pills to control your weight, you may be showing signs of a serious eating disorder and should consult your doctor or another responsible adult right away. If you smoke, which raises your chance of cancer, heart disease, and other health issues, stop as soon as you can.

If you feel like you should lose weight consult a health care professional first External link. If you need to reduce weight, a doctor or nutritionist may be able to advise you on how to do so healthily.

Select wholesome foods and beverages.

Controlling your eating habits entails choosing the foods and drinks you consume, as well as

how much of each. Try to
substitute fruits, vegetables,
whole grains, low-fat proteins,
and fat-free or low-fat dairy
products for items that are
heavy in sugar, salt, and
unhealthy fats.

Veggies and fruits

Ensure that fruits and
vegetables make up half of
your plate. Vegetables that are
dark green, red, or orange are
rich in essential nutrients like
vitamin C, calcium, and fiber.
To include additional
vegetables in your lunch, just
top your sandwich with tomato
and spinach—or any other
available greens that you
choose.

Grains

In place of cereals made with
refined grains, white bread,
and white rice, choose whole
grains such as whole-wheat
bread, brown rice, oatmeal,
and cereal.

Pick whole grains such as
whole-wheat bread, brown
rice, oatmeal, and cereal made
from whole grains.

Boost your protein intake with
low-fat or lean meats like

turkey or chicken as well as other high-protein foods like seafood, egg whites, beans, nuts, and tofu.

a dairy product

Use milk products that are fat-free or low-fat to strengthen your bones. Choose lactose-free milk or soy milk with additional calcium if you have trouble digesting lactose, a substance found in milk that can give you bloating or gas. Yogurt that is low in fat or fat-free is also a good source of dairy products.

Tips for Eating Well

Limit your intake of items like cookies, candies, frozen desserts, chips, and fries because they frequently include high levels of sugar, bad fats, and salt.

Try refueling with a pear, apple, or banana, a small bag of baby carrots, or hummus with sliced vegetables for a quick snack.

Avoid adding sugar to your meals and beverages.

Avoid sugary beverages and go for fat-free or low-fat milk instead. The additional sugars in soda, energy drinks, sweet tea, and some juices are a source of extra calories. The American Dietary Guidelines, 2020–2025 It's recommended that added sugars make up no more than 10% of your daily calories (external link).

Fats

Your diet should contain fat in moderation. Your body needs fat to expand and grow, and it may even keep your skin and hair healthy. However, compared to protein or carbohydrates, fats have more calories per gram, and some are unhealthy.

Some fats are healthier for you than others, such as plant-based oils that are liquid at room temperature. Avocados, olives, almonds, seeds, and seafood such as salmon and tuna fish are examples of foods that contain beneficial oils. Butter, stick margarine, and lard are examples of solid fats that are solid at room temperature. These lipids frequently contain unhealthy saturated and trans fats. Additionally, fatty meats,

cheese, and other dairy
products prepared from whole
milk are foods that include
saturated fats. Eat less of the
items that are commonly high
in saturated and trans fats,
such as fried chicken,
cheeseburgers, and fries.
Consider a lean-meat, turkey,
or veggie burger or a turkey
sandwich with mustard.
Avocados, olives, almonds,
seeds, and seafood such as
salmon and tuna fish are
examples of foods that contain
beneficial oils.
A limited amount of sodium,
which is primarily included in
salt, is required by your body.
However, consuming too much
sodium through your food and
beverages can cause your blood
pressure to increase, which is
bad for both your heart and
the rest of your body. In order
to avoid health issues as you
age, it's crucial to monitor your
blood pressure and heart
health today, even though
you're still a teen

Puberty is a key stage in the transition from childhood to adulthood. It is a normal part of growing up, and each person's experience of it is unique.

Puberty can be a challenging and confusing time. Knowing what to expect and why these changes happen can help a person feel more in control as they go through it.

This stage of life involves many physical and psychological changes, which result from shifts in hormone levels.

Puberty usually begins between the ages of 8 and 14. It tends to happen in females earlier than in males.

This article gives an overview of puberty, including what changes to expect, when they happen, and why.

What is puberty?

Image Source/Getty Images

During puberty, the body goes through many internal and external changes. Among other

things, this is the time when a person:
reaches their adult height and body proportions
develops external sex characteristics
becomes able to reproduce
The physical and psychological changes of puberty happen slowly over time. They typically begin between the ages of 8–13 in females and 9–14 in males.
Puberty lasts throughout the teenage years. A person may be 20 years old by the time all the changes take place.
What happens during puberty?
Puberty begins when an area of the brain called the hypothalamus starts signaling to the rest of the body that it is time to develop adult characteristics.
It sends these signals through hormones, which cause reproductive organs — the ovaries in females and the testes in males — to produce a range of other hormones.

These hormones cause growth
and changes in various parts of
the body, including the:
external reproductive organs
breast tissue
skin
muscles
bones
hair
brain
The skin becomes oily and the
body produces more sweat.
Many people develop some
form of acne. Some people
start using deodorant.
Changes in hormones also
affect the person's emotions
and thoughts. Puberty usually
has the following psychological
effects:
heightened emotions
frequently changing emotions
the start of sexual thoughts and
desires
the start of sexual and
romantic attractions to others
During puberty, many people
begin to explore their sexuality
and start to figure out whether
they are homosexual, bisexual,
heterosexual, or have another
identity. This is totally normal,

and each person's experience is different.

Not everyone will have feelings of attraction for others, and this is nothing to worry about either. People who do not develop sexual attraction may choose to identify as asexual. During puberty, some people begin to notice that their gender identity — how much they feel like a girl, a boy, or neither — does not match their body. If this happens, the physical changes of puberty can cause emotional distress known as gender dysphoria.

Hormone changes

Many changes that occur during puberty are related to shifting hormone levels. Some main hormones related to puberty are:

Testosterone. This is a primary sex hormone in males, and it gives rise to male traits, such as a deeper voice, facial hair, and muscle development.

Testosterone also plays a role in female development, to a lesser extent than in males.

Dihydrotestosterone. Called DHT, this hormone is more

powerful than testosterone and present in much higher amounts during puberty. It initiates puberty in males and may also help start puberty in females.

Estrogen. This is a primary sex hormone in females. It promotes the growth of the uterus and breast tissue.

Growth hormone. The levels of this increase during puberty, causing growth spurts in the bones and muscles, along with a rapid increase in height. A slower height increase, of less than 2 inches per year, may signal a hormone deficiency.

Estradiol. This is present in males and females. In females, the levels of estradiol rise earlier and remain higher after puberty.

Puberty in females

One of the first signs of puberty in females tends to be a breast bud, a small amount of firm tissue under the nipple. Periods typically begin around 2 years after breast development — at the age of about 12.5, on average. Along with periods, people may experience symptoms of premenstrual syndrome, known as PMS.

Emotions may fluctuate more around the time of a period, due to natural variations in hormone levels during the menstrual cycle.

Other signs of puberty include the start of vaginal discharge, body odor, and hair growing in the pubic area, under the arms, and on the legs.

Often, the hips widen, the waist becomes proportionally smaller, and extra fat develops around the stomach and buttocks. But all bodies develop differently during this time, and there is no "normal." Each person develops their unique size and shape

MANAGING MY RELATIONSHIPS

Your parental relationships, customs, and obligations as an adolescent.

Located here:

Adolescence's effects on parental and family relationships

Why do young children and adolescents require families and parents

fostering wholesome familial connections with teenagers:

Adolescence's effects on parental and family relationships

Teenagers need parent and family support just as much as they did when they were younger, even though their relationships with them alter as they go through puberty.

Parents' primary responsibilities as children are to guide and nurture them. Parents may now discover that their relationship with their children is evolving toward greater equality.

Parents provide their children with physical and financial assistance, as well as caring, emotional support, security, and safety. Even though their attitude or behavior may occasionally send a different message, a child will still love you and want you to be a part of their lives.

Most teen girls and their families experience some ups

and downs during this time, but as youngsters age, things typically get better by late adolescence. Family ties also tend to endure throughout. Why do young children and adolescents require families and parents

A teen girl's adolescence might be challenging because she is going through both rapid bodily changes and emotional ups and downs. Young folks are still figuring things out and aren't always sure where they fit. Peer pressure can also be a source of stress during adolescence.

No matter what is happening in the rest of their lives, your family provides a stable emotional basis where you were loved and welcomed as a child during this period. A family can foster and promote a child's identity, resilience, and self-assurance.

You are shielded from risky behavior like alcohol and drug use as well as issues like depression by supportive and intimate family ties. Your drive to perform well academically

can be increased by your parents' interest in and support of what you do as a teenage girl at school.
Growing up in a home with healthy relationships can be very beneficial for becoming a well-adjusted, considerate, and loving adult.
fostering healthy family relationships with teenagers:
Families can foster and improve relationships with teenagers by engaging in common, everyday activities. You and your family might find these suggestions useful.
adoration and gratitude
Parents are likely to express their love and appreciation for their teenagers. This can be as easy as giving them a high-five or saying "I love you" to them before they go to sleep each night.
family dinners
Regular family meals are a terrific time for everyone to talk about their days or exciting things that are happening or will be happening. No one will feel pressured to speak if you

encourage everyone to participate. Additionally, many families discover that meals are more pleasurable when no TV is present and all mobile devices, including tablets, are turned off.

personal time

You have the chance to maintain your relationship and enjoy each other's company when you spend time with your parents alone. It can also be an opportunity to express sentiments and thoughts. This may be as easy as taking your parents on a stroll, watching a movie, or telling them a story. Or perhaps you and your partner can engage in a regular interest like yoga or cooking.

family customs

You can set aside regular dates and special moments as a teen by using family traditions, routines, and rituals. For instance, you may plan a family movie night, a special meal or cooking session, a family game afternoon, or an evening stroll.

household obligations

Children and teenagers who are assigned home duties feel as though they are making a significant contribution to family life. These could include helping the elderly or the young members of the household, doing chores, or going shopping. It's beneficial to allow you some control over the obligations you accept. Family gatherings can aid in problem-solving. They provide an opportunity for everyone to be heard and take part in coming up with a solution.
Extra assistance
A believing family counselor or other family support service could be beneficial if you feel like your family isn't connecting.

THE BEST VERSION OF ME

But it's difficult to feel good about oneself if grownups criticize more than they compliment. Self-esteem can also be damaged by bullying and cruel taunting from siblings or peers. Harsh remarks have a way of sticking

and changing the way you view yourself. Fortunately, it need not remain that way.
the inner voice that speaks to you. How you feel about yourself is greatly influenced by the things you tell yourself. Your self-esteem suffers when you believe things like "I'm such a loser" or "I'll never make friends."
There are numerous perspectives on the same issues. "This time I didn't win, but maybe next time." "Perhaps I can meet some people," That voice sounds more upbeat. It makes you feel better. And it might end up being accurate. Sometimes, the harsh comments we hear in our heads are based on the words of others. or the difficult moments we have experienced. Sometimes the voice is merely our own harsh self-talk. But we have the power to alter the voice inside our heads. We can develop higher self-esteem. acquiring practical skills. Learning to read, add, draw, or build makes us happy. Exercise, listen to music, write

an essay, or ride a bike.
Prepare the meal and wash the car. Walk the dog and assist a friend. Every experience and accomplishment gives you a chance to feel good about yourself. Take a step back and consider your options. Allow yourself to enjoy it.

However, we can be too harsh on ourselves at times. We refuse to accept that our efforts are sufficient. We lose the possibility to boost our self-esteem if we believe that something isn't really all that nice, or perfect, or that we aren't capable of doing it well enough.

What if I don't feel confident? You can take steps to improve your self-esteem. There is always time. Here are some pointers to improve your self-worth:

Be among those who respect you. Some people behave in a way that undermines you. Others encourage you with their words and deeds. Recognize the distinctions. Select companions who will make you feel good about yourself. Find friends with whom you can be authentic. For others, be that kind of buddy.

Self-talk is constructive. Be aware of your inner voice. Is it too harsh? Do you judge yourself too harshly? Write down some of the things you tell yourself for a few days. Review your list. Would you say these things to a trustworthy friend? If not, change them to be true, just, and compassionate. Regularly read your new words. Continue doing it until having that mindset is more of a habit.

Be tolerant of imperfection. Always strive to improve yourself. However, when you believe that perfection is necessary, you cannot feel happy about anything less. Accept what you can. Allow yourself to take pleasure in that. If your demand for perfection prevents you from accepting aid, do so.

Make plans and strive toward your goals. Do things that are healthy for you if you want to feel good about yourself.

Perhaps you wish to eat a
healthier diet, exercise more,
or study more effectively.
Make a target. Then decide
how you're going to do it. Keep
to your plan. Follow your
development. Be happy with
your accomplishments thus far.
Tell yourself, "I've been
sticking to my plan to exercise
for 45 minutes each day. I'm
satisfied with it. I'm confident I
can continue."
Concentrate on the positives.
Are you so accustomed to
discussing issues that they have
become your only focus? It's
simple to become preoccupied
with what's wrong. But if you
don't counter it with the
positive, it just makes you feel
awful. The next time you find
yourself complaining about
yourself or your day, catch
yourself. Instead, look for
something that worked.
Give and assist. One of the best
methods to increase self-esteem
is to give. Tutor a classmate,
participate in local cleanups or
go on a charity walk. assist at
home or in the classroom.
Make being fair and kind a

habit. Make an effort to behave in a way that makes you proud of who you are. Your self-esteem will rise when you make a difference, no matter how tiny.

CONCLUSION